To

_____

From

_____

Date

_____

The joy of the LORD is your strength.
Nehemiah 8:10

Christian art gifts®

© Christian Art Gifts, RSA
Christian Art Gifts Inc., IL, USA
Printed in Vietnam

The path of the just is as the shining light,
that shineth more and more unto the perfect day.

~ Proverbs 4:18

Arise, shine; for thy light is come, and
the glory of the LORD is risen upon thee.

~ Isaiah 60:1

The name of the Lord is a strong tower:
the righteous runneth into it, and is safe.
~ *Proverbs 18:10*

"Blessed are the pure in heart: for they shall see God."
~ *Matthew 5:8*

_____

For the eyes of the Lord are over the righteous,
and His ears are open unto their prayers.
~ 1 Peter 3:12

_____

Blessed is every one that feareth the LORD; that walketh
in His ways. For thou shalt eat the labour of thine hands:
happy shalt thou be, and it shall be well with thee.

~ *Psalm 128:1-2*

The LORD is good to all: and His tender
mercies are over all His works.

~ Psalm 145:9

_____

Being confident of this very thing, that He which hath begun
a good work in you will perform it until the day of Jesus Christ.
~ Philippians 1:6

And of His fulness have all we received, and grace for grace.

~ John 1:16

_____

Oh that men would praise the LORD for His goodness, and for His wonderful works to the children of men! For He satisfieth the longing soul, and filleth the hungry soul with goodness.

~ Psalm 107:8-9

And we know that all things work together for good to them that
love God, to them who are the called according to His purpose.

~ Romans 8:28

_____

For the LORD God is a sun and shield: the LORD
will give grace and glory: no good thing
will He withhold from them that walk uprightly.

~ Psalm 84:11

For the Lord is good; His mercy is everlasting;
and His truth endureth to all generations.

~ Psalm 100:5

_____

The LORD taketh pleasure in them that
fear Him, in those that hope in His mercy.
~ *Psalm 147:11*

_____

"If thou canst believe, all things are possible to him that believeth."
~ Mark 9:23

_____

Eye hath not seen, nor ear heard, neither have
entered into the heart of man, the things
which God hath prepared for them that love Him.

~ *1 Corinthians 2:9*

Behold, the eye of the LORD is upon them that
fear Him, upon them that hope in His mercy.

~ Psalm 33:18

_____

But my God shall supply all your need
according to His riches in glory by Christ Jesus.
~ *Philippians 4:19*

There are many devices in a man's heart;
nevertheless the counsel of the LORD, that shall stand.
~ Proverbs 19:21

_____

And therefore will the Lᴏʀᴅ wait, that He may
be gracious unto you, and therefore will He
be exalted, that He may have mercy upon you.

~ Isaiah 30:18

The LORD hath prepared His throne in the heavens;
and His kingdom ruleth over all.

~ Psalm 103:19

_____

Blessed be the God and Father of our Lord Jesus Christ, who hath
blessed us with all spiritual blessings in heavenly places in Christ.

~ Ephesians 1:3

Thou wilt shew me the path of life: in Thy presence is fulness
of joy; at Thy right hand there are pleasures for evermore.
~ Psalm 16:11

_____

Mercy unto you, and peace, and love, be multiplied.
~ Jude 2

_____

The blessing of the Lord, it maketh rich,
and He addeth no sorrow with it.

~ Proverbs 10:22

_____

Now the God of hope fill you with all joy and peace in believing,
that ye may abound in hope, through the power of the Holy Ghost.

~ Romans 15:13

God be merciful unto us, and bless us;
and cause His face to shine upon us.
~ Psalm 67:1

_____

Cause me to hear Thy lovingkindness in the morning;
for in Thee do I trust: cause me to know the way
wherein I should walk; for I lift up my soul unto Thee.

~ Psalm 143:8

Cast thy burden upon the LORD, and He shall sustain
thee: He shall never suffer the righteous to be moved.

~ Psalm 55:22

The LORD shall preserve thee from all evil: He shall
preserve thy soul. The LORD shall preserve thy going out and
thy coming in from this time forth, and even for evermore.

~ Psalm 121:7-8

Trust in the LORD with all thine heart; and lean
not unto thine own understanding. In all thy ways
acknowledge Him, and He shall direct thy paths.

~ Proverbs 3:5-6

_____

Rejoice evermore. Pray without ceasing.
In every thing give thanks: for this is the
will of God in Christ Jesus concerning you.

~ *1 Thessalonians 5:16-18*

The path of the just is as the shining light,
that shineth more and more unto the perfect day.
~ *Proverbs 4:18*

Arise, shine; for thy light is come, and
the glory of the LORD is risen upon thee.

~ Isaiah 60:1

The name of the Lord is a strong tower:
the righteous runneth into it, and is safe.
~ Proverbs 18:10

_____

"Blessed are the pure in heart: for they shall see God."
~ Matthew 5:8

For the eyes of the Lord are over the righteous,
and His ears are open unto their prayers.

~ 1 Peter 3:12

_____

Blessed is every one that feareth the LORD; that walketh
in His ways. For thou shalt eat the labour of thine hands:
happy shalt thou be, and it shall be well with thee.

~ Psalm 128:1-2

The LORD is good to all: and His tender
mercies are over all His works.

~ Psalm 145:9

_____

Being confident of this very thing, that He which hath begun
a good work in you will perform it until the day of Jesus Christ.
~ Philippians 1:6

And of His fulness have all we received, and grace for grace.

~ John 1:16

_____

Oh that men would praise the Lord for His goodness, and for His wonderful works to the children of men! For He satisfieth the longing soul, and filleth the hungry soul with goodness.

~ Psalm 107:8-9

And we know that all things work together for good to them that
love God, to them who are the called according to His purpose.

~ Romans 8:28

_____

For the LORD God is a sun and shield: the LORD
will give grace and glory: no good thing
will He withhold from them that walk uprightly.

~ Psalm 84:11

For the LORD is good; His mercy is everlasting;
and His truth endureth to all generations.

~ Psalm 100:5

_____

The LORD taketh pleasure in them that
fear Him, in those that hope in His mercy.
~ Psalm 147:11

"If thou canst believe, all things are possible to him that believeth."
~ Mark 9:23

_____

Eye hath not seen, nor ear heard, neither have
entered into the heart of man, the things
which God hath prepared for them that love Him.
~ 1 Corinthians 2:9

Behold, the eye of the LORD is upon them that
fear Him, upon them that hope in His mercy.

~ Psalm 33:18

_____

But my God shall supply all your need
according to His riches in glory by Christ Jesus.
~ Philippians 4:19

There are many devices in a man's heart;
nevertheless the counsel of the LORD, that shall stand.

~ Proverbs 19:21

_____

And therefore will the LORD wait, that He may
be gracious unto you, and therefore will He
be exalted, that He may have mercy upon you.

~ *Isaiah 30:18*

The Lord hath prepared His throne in the heavens;
and His kingdom ruleth over all.

~ *Psalm 103:19*

_____

Blessed be the God and Father of our Lord Jesus Christ, who hath
blessed us with all spiritual blessings in heavenly places in Christ.

~ Ephesians 1:3

Thou wilt shew me the path of life: in Thy presence is fulness
of joy; at Thy right hand there are pleasures for evermore.

~ Psalm 16:11

_____

Mercy unto you, and peace, and love, be multiplied.
~ Jude 2

_____

_____
_____
_____
_____
_____
_____
_____
_____
_____
_____
_____
_____
_____
_____
_____
_____
_____
_____
_____
_____
_____
_____

The blessing of the LORD, it maketh rich,
and He addeth no sorrow with it.

~ *Proverbs 10:22*

_____

Now the God of hope fill you with all joy and peace in believing,
that ye may abound in hope, through the power of the Holy Ghost.

~ Romans 15:13

_____

_____
_____
_____
_____
_____
_____
_____
_____
_____
_____
_____
_____
_____
_____
_____
_____
_____
_____
_____
_____
_____
_____
_____

God be merciful unto us, and bless us;
and cause His face to shine upon us.

~ Psalm 67:1

_____

Cause me to hear Thy lovingkindness in the morning;
for in Thee do I trust: cause me to know the way
wherein I should walk; for I lift up my soul unto Thee.
~ Psalm 143:8

_____

_____
_____
_____
_____
_____
_____
_____
_____
_____
_____
_____
_____
_____
_____
_____
_____
_____
_____
_____
_____
_____
_____
_____

Cast thy burden upon the LORD, and He shall sustain
thee: He shall never suffer the righteous to be moved.

~ Psalm 55:22

_____

The LORD shall preserve thee from all evil: He shall
preserve thy soul. The LORD shall preserve thy going out and
thy coming in from this time forth, and even for evermore.

~ *Psalm 121:7-8*

Trust in the LORD with all thine heart; and lean
not unto thine own understanding. In all thy ways
acknowledge Him, and He shall direct thy paths.

~ Proverbs 3:5-6

_____

Rejoice evermore. Pray without ceasing.
In every thing give thanks: for this is the
will of God in Christ Jesus concerning you.
~ 1 Thessalonians 5:16-18

The path of the just is as the shining light,
that shineth more and more unto the perfect day.

~ Proverbs 4:18

_____

Arise, shine; for thy light is come, and
the glory of the LORD is risen upon thee.

~ *Isaiah 60:1*

The name of the LORD is a strong tower:
the righteous runneth into it, and is safe.

~ *Proverbs 18:10*

_____

"Blessed are the pure in heart: for they shall see God."
~ Matthew 5:8

For the eyes of the Lord are over the righteous,
and His ears are open unto their prayers.

~ 1 Peter 3:12

_____

Blessed is every one that feareth the LORD; that walketh
in His ways. For thou shalt eat the labour of thine hands:
happy shalt thou be, and it shall be well with thee.

~ *Psalm 128:1-2*

The Lord is good to all: and His tender
mercies are over all His works.

~ *Psalm 145:9*

_____

Being confident of this very thing, that He which hath begun
a good work in you will perform it until the day of Jesus Christ.
~ *Philippians 1:6*

And of His fulness have all we received, and grace for grace.

~ John 1:16

_____

Oh that men would praise the Lᴏʀᴅ for His goodness, and for His wonderful works to the children of men! For He satisfieth the longing soul, and filleth the hungry soul with goodness.

~ Psalm 107:8-9

And we know that all things work together for good to them that
love God, to them who are the called according to His purpose.

~ Romans 8:28

_____

For the LORD God is a sun and shield: the LORD
will give grace and glory: no good thing
will He withhold from them that walk uprightly.

~ Psalm 84:11

_____

For the LORD is good; His mercy is everlasting;
and His truth endureth to all generations.
~ *Psalm 100:5*

_____

The LORD taketh pleasure in them that
fear Him, in those that hope in His mercy.
~ *Psalm 147:11*

"If thou canst believe, all things are possible to him that believeth."
~ Mark 9:23

_____

Eye hath not seen, nor ear heard, neither have
entered into the heart of man, the things
which God hath prepared for them that love Him.

~ *1 Corinthians 2:9*

Behold, the eye of the Lord is upon them that
fear Him, upon them that hope in His mercy.
~ Psalm 33:18

_____

But my God shall supply all your need
according to His riches in glory by Christ Jesus.
~ *Philippians 4:19*

There are many devices in a man's heart;
nevertheless the counsel of the LORD, that shall stand.

~ Proverbs 19:21

_____

And therefore will the Lᴏʀᴅ wait, that He may
be gracious unto you, and therefore will He
be exalted, that He may have mercy upon you.
~ Isaiah 30:18

The LORD hath prepared His throne in the heavens;
and His kingdom ruleth over all.

~ Psalm 103:19

_____

_____

_____

_____

_____

_____

_____

_____

_____

_____

_____

_____

_____

_____

_____

_____

_____

_____

_____

_____

_____

_____

_____

Blessed be the God and Father of our Lord Jesus Christ, who hath
blessed us with all spiritual blessings in heavenly places in Christ.

~ Ephesians 1:3

Thou wilt shew me the path of life: in Thy presence is fulness
of joy; at Thy right hand there are pleasures for evermore.

~ Psalm 16:11

_____

Mercy unto you, and peace, and love, be multiplied.
~ *Jude 2*

The blessing of the Lord, it maketh rich,
and He addeth no sorrow with it.

~ *Proverbs 10:22*

Now the God of hope fill you with all joy and peace in believing,
that ye may abound in hope, through the power of the Holy Ghost.
~ Romans 15:13

God be merciful unto us, and bless us;
and cause His face to shine upon us.

~ Psalm 67:1

_____

Cause me to hear Thy lovingkindness in the morning;
for in Thee do I trust: cause me to know the way
wherein I should walk; for I lift up my soul unto Thee.

~ Psalm 143:8

_____

_____
_____
_____
_____
_____
_____
_____
_____
_____
_____
_____
_____
_____
_____
_____
_____
_____
_____
_____
_____
_____
_____
_____

Cast thy burden upon the LORD, and He shall sustain
thee: He shall never suffer the righteous to be moved.

~ Psalm 55:22

_____

_____

_____

_____

_____

_____

_____

_____

_____

_____

_____

_____

_____

_____

_____

_____

_____

_____

_____

_____

_____

_____

_____

_____

The LORD shall preserve thee from all evil: He shall preserve thy soul. The LORD shall preserve thy going out and thy coming in from this time forth, and even for evermore.

~ Psalm 121:7-8

Trust in the Lord with all thine heart; and lean
not unto thine own understanding. In all thy ways
acknowledge Him, and He shall direct thy paths.

~ Proverbs 3:5-6

_____

Rejoice evermore. Pray without ceasing.
In every thing give thanks: for this is the
will of God in Christ Jesus concerning you.
~ *1 Thessalonians 5:16-18*

The path of the just is as the shining light,
that shineth more and more unto the perfect day.
~ Proverbs 4:18

_____

Arise, shine; for thy light is come, and
the glory of the LORD is risen upon thee.
~ Isaiah 60:1

_____

_____

_____

_____

_____

_____

_____

_____

_____

_____

_____

_____

_____

_____

_____

_____

_____

_____

_____

_____

_____

_____

The name of the LORD is a strong tower:
the righteous runneth into it, and is safe.

~ Proverbs 18:10

_____

"Blessed are the pure in heart: for they shall see God."
~ *Matthew 5:8*

_____

_____
_____
_____
_____
_____
_____
_____
_____
_____
_____
_____
_____
_____
_____
_____
_____
_____
_____
_____
_____
_____
_____
_____

For the eyes of the Lord are over the righteous,
and His ears are open unto their prayers.

~ 1 Peter 3:12

_____

Blessed is every one that feareth the LORD; that walketh
in His ways. For thou shalt eat the labour of thine hands:
happy shalt thou be, and it shall be well with thee.

~ *Psalm 128:1-2*

The LORD is good to all: and His tender
mercies are over all His works.

~ Psalm 145:9

_____

_____

_____

_____

_____

_____

_____

_____

_____

_____

_____

_____

_____

_____

_____

_____

_____

_____

_____

_____

_____

_____

_____

_____

Being confident of this very thing, that He which hath begun
a good work in you will perform it until the day of Jesus Christ.

~ Philippians 1:6

And of His fulness have all we received, and grace for grace.

~ John 1:16

_____

Oh that men would praise the LORD for His goodness, and for
His wonderful works to the children of men! For He satisfieth
the longing soul, and filleth the hungry soul with goodness.

~ Psalm 107:8-9

And we know that all things work together for good to them that
love God, to them who are the called according to His purpose.

~ Romans 8:28

_____

For the Lord God is a sun and shield: the Lord
will give grace and glory: no good thing
will He withhold from them that walk uprightly.

~ Psalm 84:11

_____

_____
_____
_____
_____
_____
_____
_____
_____
_____
_____
_____
_____
_____
_____
_____
_____
_____
_____
_____
_____
_____
_____
_____

For the LORD is good; His mercy is everlasting;
and His truth endureth to all generations.

~ *Psalm 100:5*

_____

_____

_____

_____

_____

_____

_____

_____

_____

_____

_____

_____

_____

_____

_____

_____

_____

_____

_____

_____

_____

_____

_____

_____

The LORD taketh pleasure in them that
fear Him, in those that hope in His mercy.

~ Psalm 147:11

"If thou canst believe, all things are possible to him that believeth."
~ *Mark 9:23*

_____

Eye hath not seen, nor ear heard, neither have
entered into the heart of man, the things
which God hath prepared for them that love Him.

~ 1 Corinthians 2:9

Behold, the eye of the LORD is upon them that
fear Him, upon them that hope in His mercy.

~ Psalm 33:18

_____

But my God shall supply all your need
according to His riches in glory by Christ Jesus.
~ *Philippians 4:19*

There are many devices in a man's heart;
nevertheless the counsel of the LORD, that shall stand.
~ Proverbs 19:21

And therefore will the LORD wait, that He may
be gracious unto you, and therefore will He
be exalted, that He may have mercy upon you.

~ Isaiah 30:18

The LORD hath prepared His throne in the heavens;
and His kingdom ruleth over all.

~ Psalm 103:19

_____

Blessed be the God and Father of our Lord Jesus Christ, who hath
blessed us with all spiritual blessings in heavenly places in Christ.

~ Ephesians 1:3

Thou wilt shew me the path of life: in Thy presence is fulness
of joy; at Thy right hand there are pleasures for evermore.

~ Psalm 16:11

Mercy unto you, and peace, and love, be multiplied.

~ Jude 2

_____

_____

_____

_____

_____

_____

_____

_____

_____

_____

_____

_____

_____

_____

_____

_____

_____

_____

_____

_____

_____

_____

_____

The blessing of the Lord, it maketh rich,
and He addeth no sorrow with it.

~ Proverbs 10:22

_____

Now the God of hope fill you with all joy and peace in believing,
that ye may abound in hope, through the power of the Holy Ghost.

~ Romans 15:13

God be merciful unto us, and bless us;
and cause His face to shine upon us.

~ Psalm 67:1

_____

Cause me to hear Thy lovingkindness in the morning;
for in Thee do I trust: cause me to know the way
wherein I should walk; for I lift up my soul unto Thee.

~ Psalm 143:8

Cast thy burden upon the LORD, and He shall sustain
thee: He shall never suffer the righteous to be moved.

~ Psalm 55:22

_____

The LORD shall preserve thee from all evil: He shall
preserve thy soul. The LORD shall preserve thy going out and
thy coming in from this time forth, and even for evermore.

~ Psalm 121:7-8

Trust in the L ORD with all thine heart; and lean
not unto thine own understanding. In all thy ways
acknowledge Him, and He shall direct thy paths.

~ Proverbs 3:5-6

_____

Rejoice evermore. Pray without ceasing.
In every thing give thanks: for this is the
will of God in Christ Jesus concerning you.
~ 1 Thessalonians 5:16-18

The path of the just is as the shining light,
that shineth more and more unto the perfect day.
~ *Proverbs 4:18*

_____

Arise, shine; for thy light is come, and
the glory of the LORD is risen upon thee.
~ *Isaiah 60:1*

The name of the LORD is a strong tower:
the righteous runneth into it, and is safe.
~ Proverbs 18:10

_____

"Blessed are the pure in heart: for they shall see God."
~ Matthew 5:8

For the eyes of the Lord are over the righteous,
and His ears are open unto their prayers.

~ 1 Peter 3:12

_____

Blessed is every one that feareth the LORD; that walketh
in His ways. For thou shalt eat the labour of thine hands:
happy shalt thou be, and it shall be well with thee.

~ Psalm 128:1-2

The Lord is good to all: and His tender
mercies are over all His works.

~ Psalm 145:9

_____

Being confident of this very thing, that He which hath begun
a good work in you will perform it until the day of Jesus Christ.
~ Philippians 1:6

And of His fulness have all we received, and grace for grace.

~ John 1:16

_____

Oh that men would praise the Lᴏʀᴅ for His goodness, and for His wonderful works to the children of men! For He satisfieth the longing soul, and filleth the hungry soul with goodness.

~ Psalm 107:8-9

And we know that all things work together for good to them that
love God, to them who are the called according to His purpose.

~ Romans 8:28

_____

For the Lord God is a sun and shield: the Lord
will give grace and glory: no good thing
will He withhold from them that walk uprightly.

~ Psalm 84:11

For the Lord is good; His mercy is everlasting;
and His truth endureth to all generations.
~ Psalm 100:5

_____

The LORD taketh pleasure in them that
fear Him, in those that hope in His mercy.

~ Psalm 147:11

"If thou canst believe, all things are possible to him that believeth."
~ *Mark 9:23*

_____

Eye hath not seen, nor ear heard, neither have
entered into the heart of man, the things
which God hath prepared for them that love Him.

~ *1 Corinthians 2:9*

Behold, the eye of the Lord is upon them that
fear Him, upon them that hope in His mercy.

~ Psalm 33:18

_____

_____

_____

_____

_____

_____

_____

_____

_____

_____

_____

_____

_____

_____

_____

_____

_____

_____

_____

_____

_____

But my God shall supply all your need
according to His riches in glory by Christ Jesus.
~ *Philippians 4:19*

There are many devices in a man's heart;
nevertheless the counsel of the LORD, that shall stand.

~ Proverbs 19:21

_____

And therefore will the LORD wait, that He may
be gracious unto you, and therefore will He
be exalted, that He may have mercy upon you.
~ Isaiah 30:18

The LORD hath prepared His throne in the heavens;
and His kingdom ruleth over all.
~ Psalm 103:19

_____

Blessed be the God and Father of our Lord Jesus Christ, who hath blessed us with all spiritual blessings in heavenly places in Christ.

~ Ephesians 1:3

Thou wilt shew me the path of life: in Thy presence is fulness
of joy; at Thy right hand there are pleasures for evermore.

~ Psalm 16:11

_____

Mercy unto you, and peace, and love, be multiplied.
~ *Jude 2*

The blessing of the Lord, it maketh rich,
and He addeth no sorrow with it.

~ Proverbs 10:22

_____

Now the God of hope fill you with all joy and peace in believing,
that ye may abound in hope, through the power of the Holy Ghost.

~ Romans 15:13

God be merciful unto us, and bless us;
and cause His face to shine upon us.

~ Psalm 67:1

_____

Cause me to hear Thy lovingkindness in the morning;
for in Thee do I trust: cause me to know the way
wherein I should walk; for I lift up my soul unto Thee.
~ *Psalm 143:8*

Cast thy burden upon the LORD, and He shall sustain
thee: He shall never suffer the righteous to be moved.

~ Psalm 55:22

_____

The LORD shall preserve thee from all evil: He shall
preserve thy soul. The LORD shall preserve thy going out and
thy coming in from this time forth, and even for evermore.

~ Psalm 121:7-8

Trust in the L<small>ORD</small> with all thine heart; and lean
not unto thine own understanding. In all thy ways
acknowledge Him, and He shall direct thy paths.

~ Proverbs 3:5-6

_____

Rejoice evermore. Pray without ceasing.
In every thing give thanks: for this is the
will of God in Christ Jesus concerning you.

~ 1 Thessalonians 5:16-18

The path of the just is as the shining light,
that shineth more and more unto the perfect day.

~ Proverbs 4:18

_____

Arise, shine; for thy light is come, and
the glory of the LORD is risen upon thee.
~ *Isaiah 60:1*

The name of the LORD is a strong tower:
the righteous runneth into it, and is safe.
~ *Proverbs 18:10*

_____

"Blessed are the pure in heart: for they shall see God."
~ Matthew 5:8

For the eyes of the Lord are over the righteous,
and His ears are open unto their prayers.
~ 1 Peter 3:12

_____

Blessed is every one that feareth the Lord; that walketh
in His ways. For thou shalt eat the labour of thine hands:
happy shalt thou be, and it shall be well with thee.

~ *Psalm 128:1-2*

The LORD is good to all: and His tender
mercies are over all His works.
~ Psalm 145:9

_____

Being confident of this very thing, that He which hath begun
a good work in you will perform it until the day of Jesus Christ.
~ *Philippians 1:6*

And of His fulness have all we received, and grace for grace.
~ John 1:16

_____

Oh that men would praise the LORD for His goodness, and for
His wonderful works to the children of men! For He satisfieth
the longing soul, and filleth the hungry soul with goodness.

~ Psalm 107:8-9

And we know that all things work together for good to them that love God, to them who are the called according to His purpose.
~ *Romans 8:28*

For the LORD God is a sun and shield: the LORD
will give grace and glory: no good thing
will He withhold from them that walk uprightly.

~ Psalm 84:11

For the LORD is good; His mercy is everlasting;
and His truth endureth to all generations.

~ Psalm 100:5

The LORD taketh pleasure in them that
fear Him, in those that hope in His mercy.

~ Psalm 147:11

"If thou canst believe, all things are possible to him that believeth."

~ Mark 9:23

_____

Eye hath not seen, nor ear heard, neither have
entered into the heart of man, the things
which God hath prepared for them that love Him.

~ 1 Corinthians 2:9

Behold, the eye of the LORD is upon them that
fear Him, upon them that hope in His mercy.

~ Psalm 33:18

_____

But my God shall supply all your need
according to His riches in glory by Christ Jesus.
~ Philippians 4:19

There are many devices in a man's heart;
nevertheless the counsel of the LORD, that shall stand.
~ Proverbs 19:21

_____

And therefore will the LORD wait, that He may
be gracious unto you, and therefore will He
be exalted, that He may have mercy upon you.

~ Isaiah 30:18

The LORD hath prepared His throne in the heavens;
and His kingdom ruleth over all.
~ Psalm 103:19

_____

_____

_____

_____

_____

_____

_____

_____

_____

_____

_____

_____

_____

_____

_____

_____

_____

_____

_____

_____

_____

_____

_____

Blessed be the God and Father of our Lord Jesus Christ, who hath
blessed us with all spiritual blessings in heavenly places in Christ.

~ Ephesians 1:3

Thou wilt shew me the path of life: in Thy presence is fulness
of joy; at Thy right hand there are pleasures for evermore.

~ *Psalm 16:11*

_____

Mercy unto you, and peace, and love, be multiplied.
~ *Jude 2*

The blessing of the Lord, it maketh rich,
and He addeth no sorrow with it.

~ Proverbs 10:22

Now the God of hope fill you with all joy and peace in believing,
that ye may abound in hope, through the power of the Holy Ghost.

~ Romans 15:13

God be merciful unto us, and bless us;
and cause His face to shine upon us.

~ Psalm 67:1

_____

Cause me to hear Thy lovingkindness in the morning;
for in Thee do I trust: cause me to know the way
wherein I should walk; for I lift up my soul unto Thee.

~ Psalm 143:8

Cast thy burden upon the LORD, and He shall sustain
thee: He shall never suffer the righteous to be moved.

~ *Psalm 55:22*

_____

The LORD shall preserve thee from all evil: He shall
preserve thy soul. The LORD shall preserve thy going out and
thy coming in from this time forth, and even for evermore.

~ Psalm 121:7-8

Trust in the Lord with all thine heart; and lean
not unto thine own understanding. In all thy ways
acknowledge Him, and He shall direct thy paths.

~ Proverbs 3:5-6

_____

_____
_____
_____
_____
_____
_____
_____
_____
_____
_____
_____
_____
_____
_____
_____
_____
_____
_____
_____
_____
_____
_____
_____

Rejoice evermore. Pray without ceasing.
In every thing give thanks: for this is the
will of God in Christ Jesus concerning you.
~ *1 Thessalonians 5:16-18*

The path of the just is as the shining light,
that shineth more and more unto the perfect day.
~ *Proverbs 4:18*

Arise, shine; for thy light is come, and
the glory of the LORD is risen upon thee.

~ Isaiah 60:1

The name of the LORD is a strong tower:
the righteous runneth into it, and is safe.
~ Proverbs 18:10

_____

"Blessed are the pure in heart: for they shall see God."
~ Matthew 5:8

For the eyes of the Lord are over the righteous,
and His ears are open unto their prayers.

~ 1 Peter 3:12

_____

Blessed is every one that feareth the LORD; that walketh
in His ways. For thou shalt eat the labour of thine hands:
happy shalt thou be, and it shall be well with thee.

~ Psalm 128:1-2

The LORD is good to all: and His tender
mercies are over all His works.

~ Psalm 145:9

_____

Being confident of this very thing, that He which hath begun
a good work in you will perform it until the day of Jesus Christ.
~ *Philippians 1:6*

And of His fulness have all we received, and grace for grace.

~ John 1:16

_____

Oh that men would praise the LORD for His goodness, and for
His wonderful works to the children of men! For He satisfieth
the longing soul, and filleth the hungry soul with goodness.

~ *Psalm 107:8-9*

And we know that all things work together for good to them that
love God, to them who are the called according to His purpose.

~ Romans 8:28

_____

For the Lord God is a sun and shield: the Lord
will give grace and glory: no good thing
will He withhold from them that walk uprightly.

~ Psalm 84:11

For the LORD is good; His mercy is everlasting;
and His truth endureth to all generations.

~ *Psalm 100:5*

The LORD taketh pleasure in them that
fear Him, in those that hope in His mercy.

~ Psalm 147:11

"If thou canst believe, all things are possible to him that believeth."

~ Mark 9:23

_____

Eye hath not seen, nor ear heard, neither have
entered into the heart of man, the things
which God hath prepared for them that love Him.

~ 1 Corinthians 2:9

Behold, the eye of the Lᴏʀᴅ is upon them that
fear Him, upon them that hope in His mercy.

~ Psalm 33:18

_____

_____
_____
_____
_____
_____
_____
_____
_____
_____
_____
_____
_____
_____
_____
_____
_____
_____
_____
_____
_____
_____
_____

But my God shall supply all your need
according to His riches in glory by Christ Jesus.
~ Philippians 4:19

There are many devices in a man's heart;
nevertheless the counsel of the LORD, that shall stand.

~ Proverbs 19:21

_____

And therefore will the LORD wait, that He may
be gracious unto you, and therefore will He
be exalted, that He may have mercy upon you.

~ Isaiah 30:18

_____

_____

_____

_____

_____

_____

_____

_____

_____

_____

_____

_____

_____

_____

_____

_____

_____

_____

_____

_____

_____

_____

_____

The LORD hath prepared His throne in the heavens;
and His kingdom ruleth over all.

~ Psalm 103:19

_____

Blessed be the God and Father of our Lord Jesus Christ, who hath
blessed us with all spiritual blessings in heavenly places in Christ.

~ Ephesians 1:3

Thou wilt shew me the path of life: in Thy presence is fulness
of joy; at Thy right hand there are pleasures for evermore.

~ Psalm 16:11

_____

Mercy unto you, and peace, and love, be multiplied.
~ Jude 2

The blessing of the Lord, it maketh rich,
and He addeth no sorrow with it.

~ *Proverbs 10:22*

_____

Now the God of hope fill you with all joy and peace in believing,
that ye may abound in hope, through the power of the Holy Ghost.
~ *Romans 15:13*

God be merciful unto us, and bless us;
and cause His face to shine upon us.

~ Psalm 67:1

_____

Cause me to hear Thy lovingkindness in the morning;
for in Thee do I trust: cause me to know the way
wherein I should walk; for I lift up my soul unto Thee.

~ Psalm 143:8

_____

_____
_____
_____
_____
_____
_____
_____
_____
_____
_____
_____
_____
_____
_____
_____
_____
_____
_____
_____
_____
_____
_____
_____
_____

Cast thy burden upon the LORD, and He shall sustain
thee: He shall never suffer the righteous to be moved.

~ Psalm 55:22

The LORD shall preserve thee from all evil: He shall preserve thy soul. The LORD shall preserve thy going out and thy coming in from this time forth, and even for evermore.

~ *Psalm 121:7-8*

Trust in the Lord with all thine heart; and lean
not unto thine own understanding. In all thy ways
acknowledge Him, and He shall direct thy paths.

~ *Proverbs 3:5-6*

_____

Rejoice evermore. Pray without ceasing.
In every thing give thanks: for this is the
will of God in Christ Jesus concerning you.
~ *1 Thessalonians 5:16-18*

The path of the just is as the shining light,
that shineth more and more unto the perfect day.

~ Proverbs 4:18

_____

Arise, shine; for thy light is come, and
the glory of the Lord is risen upon thee.
~ Isaiah 60:1

The name of the LORD is a strong tower:
the righteous runneth into it, and is safe.
~ Proverbs 18:10

_____

"Blessed are the pure in heart: for they shall see God."
~ Matthew 5:8

For the eyes of the Lord are over the righteous,
and His ears are open unto their prayers.
~ 1 Peter 3:12

_____

Blessed is every one that feareth the Lord; that walketh
in His ways. For thou shalt eat the labour of thine hands:
happy shalt thou be, and it shall be well with thee.

~ Psalm 128:1-2

The LORD is good to all: and His tender
mercies are over all His works.

~ *Psalm 145:9*

_____

Being confident of this very thing, that He which hath begun
a good work in you will perform it until the day of Jesus Christ.
~ Philippians 1:6

And of His fulness have all we received, and grace for grace.

~ John 1:16

_____

Oh that men would praise the LORD for His goodness, and for His wonderful works to the children of men! For He satisfieth the longing soul, and filleth the hungry soul with goodness.

~ Psalm 107:8-9

And we know that all things work together for good to them that love God, to them who are the called according to His purpose.

~ Romans 8:28

_____

For the LORD God is a sun and shield: the LORD
will give grace and glory: no good thing
will He withhold from them that walk uprightly.

~ Psalm 84:11

For the Lord is good; His mercy is everlasting;
and His truth endureth to all generations.

~ Psalm 100:5

The LORD taketh pleasure in them that
fear Him, in those that hope in His mercy.
~ Psalm 147:11